HISTORIC
COMMUNITIES

Customs and Traditions

Bobbie Kalman & Tammy Everts

Toronto·Oxford
New York·p.d.

Crabtree Publishing Company

HISTORIC COMMUNITIES

Created by Bobbie Kalman

For my sister, Tina Everts

Editor-in-Chief
Bobbie Kalman

Writing team
Bobbie Kalman
Tammy Everts

Editors
David Schimpky
Tammy Everts
Lynda Hale
Petrina Gentile

Computer design
Lynda Hale

Photo researcher
Janine Schaub

Color separations
Book Art Inc.

Printer
Worzalla Publishing

Special thanks to
Ann Duffy and the Yankee Publishing Company, Lorraine O'Byrne and Black Creek Pioneer Village, Rose Hasner and the Metropolitan Regional Conservation Authority, and Dave Schalk (whose photo appears on page 14)

Published by
Crabtree Publishing Company

350 Fifth Avenue
Suite 3308
New York
N.Y. 10118

360 York Road, RR 4
Niagara-on-the-Lake
Ontario, Canada
L0S 1J0

73 Lime Walk
Headington
Oxford OX3 7AD
United Kingdom

Cataloging in Publication Data

Kalman, Bobbie, 1947-
    Customs and traditions

(The historic communities series)
Includes index.
ISBN 0-86505-495-9 (library bound)   ISBN 0-86505-515-7 (pbk.)
This book examines the customs and traditions of nineteenth-century North American communities.

1. North America - Social life and customs - 19th century - Juvenile literature. 2. Frontier and pioneer life - North America - Juvenile literature. I. Everts, Tammy, 1970- . II. Title. III. Series: Kalman, Bobbie, 1947- . Historic communities.

FC88.K35 1994   j390'.0971   LC 93-39882
F1021.K35 1994

Contents

Customs and traditions

Customs and traditions are a part of who we are. They are our actions, habits, values, and celebrations. Some customs and traditions are observed every day; others make special occasions mean more to us. Looking at the customs and traditions of a group of people helps us understand that group's way of life.

Cultural customs

Customs are the usual ways people behave around one another. How they say hello, the way they eat their food, and when they go to sleep can all be customs. In some countries it is customary to greet people by kissing them on both cheeks. In Japan, people bow to one another when they meet. Having a *siesta*, or nap, after lunch in Mexico, eating with chopsticks in China, and painting eggs at Easter are also customs.

(above) Hundreds of years ago a man named Martin Luther started the custom of decorating trees at Christmastime.

(below) This mother and daughter are enjoying a customary Mexican nap called a siesta.

What are traditions?

Traditions are customs that are carried out at special times and repeated generation after generation. Decorating evergreen trees is a Christmas custom, but hanging cookies on the tree may be a tradition in certain families. In some communities, filling the church with the fruits of the harvest is a Thanksgiving tradition. In many cultures, women traditionally wear white dresses on their wedding day. A family reunion is a yearly tradition with some families.

The ways of the settlers

The early settlers had many customs and traditions that might seem unusual today. One early custom involved bathing newborn babies in wine to make them strong and healthy! A Hallowe'en custom required people to sleep with leaves and dust under their pillows to help them dream about the future. Early family traditions included wearing a brooch containing the hair of a loved one who had died.

What are your customs and traditions?

With a group of friends, make a list of the customs of your cultures and the traditions of your families. Do your friends have family traditions that are different from yours? Are there some traditions that you would like to start and pass down to your children?

Eating with chopsticks has been a Chinese custom for centuries.

Celebrating the fruits of the harvest is a Thanksgiving tradition.

Community customs

Early communities were close knit. Although these close ties sometimes made people suspicious of outsiders, they also brought members of a community together. Before the days of police stations and fire departments, it was important that everyone cooperate.

No guests allowed!

In some communities it was illegal to have guests from other towns stay overnight, even if they were family members! There were laws that prevented people from selling their houses to outsiders without the permission of the whole community. The settlers worried that strangers might be dangerous criminals.

On **at-home days,** *people opened their houses to visitors from the community. Guests dropped by all day long and enjoyed sandwiches, cakes, and drinks. On other days, if people called on someone who was not at home, they left* **calling cards** *with their names printed on them.*

Watchful eyes

The **rattle-watch**, or **bell-man**, had an important job. He was a watchman who walked around the village all night long. As the sun set, he reminded people to light the lamps outside their homes. The rattle-watch called out the time and weather every hour. He was responsible for the safety of the people in the town.

The **cow-keep** was also an important member of the community. During busy summers, farmers shared the cost of hiring a man to care for all the cattle. At sunrise the cow-keep walked through town, sounding a horn to call the cows. The cattle followed him to the pasture outside the town. The cow-keep protected the cows until sunset, when he herded them home.

(below) The settlers had plenty of work to do, but they found time for fun. Sometimes groups of people met near the house of a family they were going to surprise. They then paraded to that family's house, bringing food and musical instruments with them. Dancing, singing, and eating carried on throughout the night!

*(top) Carpenters made furniture, but they also made coffins. They doubled as **undertakers**.*

*(inset) The **blacksmith** made tools and other objects from iron. In some towns he was also the **farrier** who nailed horseshoes onto animals' hooves. When someone had a decayed tooth, the blacksmith acted as the dentist and yanked out the painful molar with his pliers!*

Double duty

Many settler communities had a small population. As a result, there were not enough skilled people to perform every job that needed to be done. Most people had two or more occupations. For example, almost everyone in the community grew crops and raised animals. Even the carpenter, blacksmith, and storekeeper doubled as farmers. In the winter some farmers worked as loggers. They chopped down the trees that were cut into planks at the sawmill.

The carpenter and undertaker

The local carpenter was also the **undertaker**. An undertaker is a person who prepares people who have died for burial and arranges for the funeral. After the carpenter made the coffin, he drove the deceased to the cemetery in his **hearse**, a special wagon used for funerals.

Barber or bloodletter?

The barber was the closest person to a doctor that many communities had. He cut hair, but he also performed **bloodletting**. The settlers believed that people who were sick had "bad blood." Cutting the skin and allowing the patient to bleed was thought to cure many types of illnesses. Unfortunately, bloodletting often made the patient weaker. The barber's red-and-white striped pole advertised his bloodletting service. The red stood for blood and the white for bandages.

The miller and baker

Farmers had their wheat ground into flour at the **gristmill**. Besides grinding the wheat, the miller, who ran the gristmill, owned the bakery that made and sold bread. The miller was one of the richer and more powerful men in the community. He was often the mayor of the town.

(top) The miller kept some of the flour he ground as payment for his services. He used the extra flour to bake bread, which he sold in his bakery.

(inset) The general storekeeper sold all kinds of goods, but he or she was also the village postmaster. The mail boxes, which are shown on the left side of the picture, took up a corner of the store.

Settler Sundays

Religion was an important part of life for most settlers. Some of their religious rules and customs might seem quite different from the religious practices of today.

A family that did not go to church regularly was rare. In some very early communities, people who missed a Sunday service were put in the stocks to be ridiculed by their neighbors.

Watch what you wear!

Members of the Puritan group had strict rules about church, manners, and even clothing. Women were not allowed to have lace on their clothing, and men were not permitted to don beaver-skin hats. People who disobeyed these rules could be arrested and sent to jail!

Unusual foot-warmers

Some churches were not heated in the winter. The settlers did not think it was proper to have a stove in the church. Instead, dogs were allowed to lie across people's feet to keep the toes of their owners warm during the long sermon! The church hired **dog-pelters** to control the canine foot-warmers.

Noah's Ark

Early settler children were not allowed to work or play on Sunday. In the Bible, Sunday was called a "day of rest." People felt that children, too, had to rest—even if they didn't feel tired! Children were only permitted to play with a small wooden Noah's Ark toy because the story of Noah came from the Bible.

The Noah's Ark toy was very popular among early settler children. It was the only toy with which they were allowed to play on Sunday!

Dog-pelters *kept the dogs that warmed their owner's feet from creating problems in church. This excited pup is getting a stern warning. He might soon find himself waiting outside for his owner.*

Telling and remembering

Newspapers were not very common among the earliest settlers. People had to rely on different ways of hearing and remembering news. Some settlers had creative ways of keeping up to date on the latest happenings.

Family circulars

Since relatives often settled in different parts of the country, visits were rare. In order to stay in touch, families used **circulars** to spread the news.

*This family has just received a **circular** from relatives who live far away. They eagerly gather in the kitchen to hear the latest family news. For many people, circulars were the only way to stay in touch with distant loved ones.*

At the beginning of the month, someone took a sheet of paper, filled part of it with family news, and mailed it to a distant family. That family read the news, added more of its own, and then mailed it to another family. This continued until the circular reached the last family, which kept all the circulars to pass along to future generations. Circulars were a good way to remember family history.

Family journals

Family members were too busy to keep individual diaries, so they shared a family **journal**. The journal was similar to a circular. On Monday, Mother might write about her day, and then pass the journal along to Father on Tuesday. He would add his own news and pass the journal on to another family member. This went on until everyone had written something. Families kept these journals for many years.

(above) In the days of the early settlers, there were no photographs. Instead, family members and friends remembered one another by wearing necklaces, rings, and bracelets made with one another's hair. Sometimes the hair of a family member who had died was arranged in a beautiful design and added to a brooch. This kind of brooch was called a **mourning pin.** *It was worn on important occasions.*

(left) Convince your family or class to start a group journal. A journal is fun to write and read. It is also a good way to keep track of everyday events in your home or school.

The family Bible

Another way the settlers preserved their family history was by keeping records in the large family Bible. Inside the Bible were blank pages reserved for recording births, weddings, deaths, and other important events. Families passed down their Bibles from generation to generation.

The importance of almanacs

Each year settler families bought a new **almanac** for the home. As one saying went, "A person without an almanac is like a ship without a compass. He or she never knows what to do or when to do it."

To the settlers, the almanac was a very important book. It predicted the weather and gave information about the movement of the stars and planets. It offered advice on everything from farming and cooking to health and love. Everyone in the family had a reason to enjoy the almanac.

People looked forward to the **town crier's** *stroll through the streets. As he walked, the crier rang a bell to get people's attention. When everyone was listening, he shouted out the news. The town crier was an early news broadcaster!*

The Farmer's Almanac

The best-known almanac is *The Farmer's Almanac*, or *The Old Farmer's Almanac* (as it was later called). This popular book has been printed every year since 1793! Before radio and television existed, farmers depended on *The Farmer's Almanac* for weather forecasts for the following day, week, month, and even year! *The Farmer's Almanac*

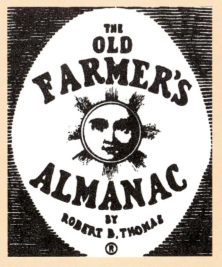

was famous for being able to predict the weather accurately. One year a mistake was made in *The Farmer's Almanac*. The almanac predicted "Rain, Hail, and Snow" for a day in the middle of July. Sure enough, rain, hail, and snow fell from the sky on that day! After that, many people believed that *The Farmer's Almanac* could never be wrong.

Predicting the weather

*The settlers believed that the wind brought different types of weather, depending on the direction from which it blew. For example, a wind from the north was believed to bring cold weather. The **weather vane** helped farmers by signaling changes in the direction of the wind.*

Watching the weather was an important part of settler life. Sun and rain are both necessary, but only in moderate amounts. Too little rain and too much sun can dry out the fields and prevent plants from growing. Too much rain can destroy a farmer's crops. Knowing when it will rain and when it will be sunny helps farmers decide when to plant. Settler farmers predicted the weather by observing animals, fish, insects, plants, and the sky. Much of what the settlers believed is considered true even today. Some farmers still use age-old ways to predict the weather!

How to read the weather

Signs of sun
Settlers thought that fair weather was coming when:
- there was heavy dew after a fair day
- the sky was red during sunset
- there was a fog or mist on the fields
- the wind slowly changed direction

Signs of rain
Settlers believed that rain was on its way when:
- a dog ate grass
- a cat washed over its ears with its paws
- a crow flew across the sky alone
- the leaves of trees turned upside down
- fish swam near the surface of the water
- flies swarmed together
- ants marched in a line
- the sky was red during sunrise
- the sky around the sun was hazy
- there was a halo around the moon (the larger the halo, the sooner the rainfall)
- the stars were extra "twinkly"

Can you predict the weather? Find and count the "weather signs" in this picture. The settlers knew that seeing one or two signs could be a coincidence, but spotting several signs was a sure way to tell if rain, snow, or good weather was on its way.

In the kitchen

No dishes to wash

Few of the earliest settlers had dinner plates made of tin or china. Instead, they ate from hollowed-out slabs of wood called **trenchers**, which were shared by two or more people. Some settlers used a **tableboard** instead of trenchers. This thick wooden tabletop had bowls carved right into it! Cleanup was simple—after each meal, the entire tabletop was lifted off and washed.

Run, dog, run!

Some settlers had a special way of cooking over a fire. They cooked large pieces of meat on a **spit**, a metal rod that ran through the roast. The spit had to be turned so that the meat would be evenly cooked. Turning the spit was a tiresome task that could take hours, so settlers trained dogs to do the job! **Turnspit dogs** were small, short-legged dogs. To turn the spit, they ran inside a dog wheel, much like a hamster that runs inside a wheel for exercise.

The settlers had some interesting tools and gadgets in their kitchens. Locate them using these illustrations as clues. Are any of these settler gadgets still used today?

trencher

a peel was used for removing hot bread from the bread oven

butter mold

18

A new taste sensation!

Water was considered an unhealthy drink. English settlers drank ale, the Dutch drank beer, and the French and Spanish drank wine. Even children drank alcohol! Eventually the settlers tried drinking water. They were surprised by how good it made them feel!

The magic of honey

The settlers believed that honey had many purposes. Besides tasting good, it was used as a cure for poisoning and bad temper. Honey was also thought to protect cows from disease. The settlers believed that keeping beehives near their homes would prevent lightning from striking their houses.

Powerful plants

The settlers thought that some plants held special powers. Women often fastened a twig from an elm tree to their churns. They didn't think butter would form without this magic twig. Many types of herbs were used for flavoring foods and curing illnesses. They were hung over the fireplace to dry.

a bellows fanned the fire

a trivet raised pots above the coals

bake oven

pestle

dog wheel

Health and cleanliness

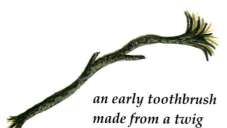

an early toothbrush made from a twig

(below) What could this doctor be doing to his patient's ear? Perhaps he is giving her an "ear-y" ant-egg cure!

The ideas the settlers had about health and cleanliness were very different from today's medical practices. One deafness cure prescribed dropping a mixture of onion juice and ant eggs in the patient's ear! A recommended earache cure suggested that the sufferer place a brass button in his or her mouth. Someone was then supposed to surprise the patient by firing a gun. This was believed to cure the pain—or scare the patient into forgetting about it!

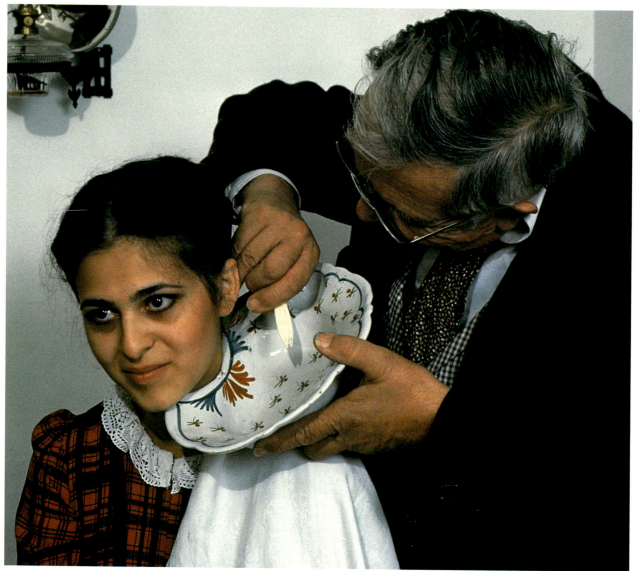

Sewn up for winter

The settlers believed that the oils that formed on dirty skin were healthy, so they made sure they didn't wash very often. Another way to preserve these oils was to be sewn into a pair of full-length long johns in the fall and cut out of them in the spring! This practice was called being "sewn up against the cold." Obviously, these stitched-up settlers did not bathe for several months!

People who caught a cold used their long johns as part of the remedy. They rubbed their entire body with goose fat and then tucked onions into their long johns! This remedy was believed to cure coughing and sneezing. Another cure for a cough was applying a hot mustard plaster to the chest.

Taking care of hair

The settlers didn't wash their hair very often, but they had other ways of keeping it "healthy." Women brushed their hair more than 100 times a day to make it shiny. To treat dandruff, they rubbed bran into their scalp. Settler men tried to cure baldness by rubbing their head with onions or with a mixture of castor oil, rosemary, and goose fat!

Blast your way to clean teeth

Toothbrushes were not common, so people had to find other ways of keeping their mouth clean. Some people brushed their teeth with frayed twigs and gunpowder! Mouthwashes were made out of everything from lemon juice to wine. Rubbing gums with wool that had been coated in honey helped get rid of bad breath, but it was not a great way to fight cavities! No wonder many settlers had toothless grins!

Doctors believed that diseases were carried in the blood. The best way to get rid of an illness was to "bleed" the patient by applying leeches to the skin!

Leeches were transported in small wooden leech barrels and stored in glass jars. No one wanted these blood-sucking creatures to get away!

Holidays

Customs and traditions are an important part of every holiday. Today we celebrate holidays with gifts, decorations, or costumes that we buy in stores. The settlers celebrated using things they found or made themselves.

Fancy floors

Many of the first settler homes had floors of hard-packed dirt. On special days the earthen floor became an unusual "carpet." The floor was

*Holding apple-peeling parties, or **bees**, was a favorite way of making a time-consuming job easy and fun. Young men and women tried to pare their apples leaving a long, curly peel, which they threw into the air. If the peel landed in the shape of a letter, it was believed to be the initial of a future husband or wife.*

swept smooth, and decorative designs were scratched onto it with a stick. The dirt carpet could have a variety of patterns, depending on the occasion. Flowers for birthdays and holly for Christmas were two common designs.

Finding the words

Valentine's Day **writers** were popular with tongue-tied young men. A writer was a book filled with romantic verses and messages. A young man used a writer when he could not think of words to express his feelings for a young woman. Some young women had writers, too. When they received a Valentine, they checked their writer to see if a young man's message was original!

Easter eggs

For the early settlers, Easter was a very religious holiday. The weeks before Easter were spent fasting and praying. On Easter Sunday people went to church. As time passed, however, new traditions, such as eating or saving Easter eggs, were added to the celebrations. The settlers believed that an egg laid on Good Friday and eaten on Easter Sunday would bring good luck for the rest of the year. Some "Good Friday" eggs were saved and used to fight sicknesses.

Predicting the future

Lumpy pillows were part of one Hallowe'en custom. Some settlers believed that, on Hallowe'en night, a person should walk backwards outdoors, pick up some dirt or grass, wrap it in paper, and put it under his or her pillow! That night the person would dream of what the future held.

Old-fashioned Valentine's Day cards were blank inside but had beautiful designs on the outside.

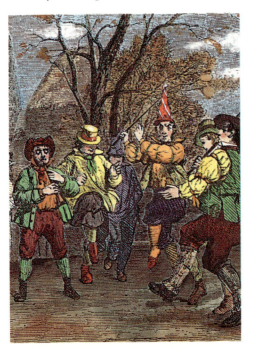

*Christmas **mumming** was a tradition brought from Europe. **Mummers**, wearing homemade costumes or disguises, paraded through the streets and visited neighbors. They sang, danced, or performed plays in exchange for food and drinks.*

Courtship and marriage

Courting and **sparking** were early words for dating. Sunday was the special day for courtship. Young men waited outside church to walk young women home.

Getting acquainted

When young men and women attended dances, parties, and bees, they carried **conversation lozenges** with them. Conversation lozenges were heart-shaped candies with romantic messages written on them. Men presented them to the women they liked. If a young woman did not give the candy back, or if she gave the young man one of her own lozenges, the two were on their way to becoming a couple.

Bride's boxes

Giving a **bride's box** was a tradition among early German settlers. When a man and woman became engaged to be married, the man gave the woman a bride's box, which was a large wooden chest. The box was used to store things the new bride would need, such as quilts, sheets, and napkins. She also used the box to save treasured keepsakes. These boxes were also known as **hope chests**.

Sweet dreams

Wedding cakes were an important part of celebrating a marriage. Hiding a nutmeg inside the cake was a wedding tradition. The person who got the slice of cake containing the nutmeg was believed to be the next to marry. If a young woman did not get the hidden nutmeg, she wrapped up a piece of cake and took it home.

Sunday afternoon was a good time for courting. Going for a carriage ride was one way to get to know someone special.

After months of courtship, a wedding was an exciting event. The bride carried a bouquet of flowers, which was believed to bring good luck to the married couple.

Women thought that sleeping with wedding cake under their pillow would make them dream about their future husbands.

The noisy charivari

Sometimes a wedding party was interrupted by a **charivari**, or **shivaree**. Groups of young men, dressed in old clothes, hats, and strange masks, "serenaded" the newlyweds. They made music with cowbells, horns, pots, and pans. The noise continued until the "musicians" were invited to join the party. Charivaris were usually good fun, but sometimes they became a noisy nuisance. Over-enthusiastic charivari participants often played pranks on the bride and groom.

The bride cut the first piece of cake and served it to her husband as a symbol of their new shared life.

*Sometimes **charivari** pranks got a little out of hand!*

A new baby

Early settlers were very excited when a baby was born. Families looked forward to having another child to love. Children were also useful. A new member of the family meant another helping hand around the house.

Sweet thoughts only, please

When a woman was pregnant, she was instructed to think only good thoughts. The settlers believed that negative or angry thoughts could harm the baby! Good thoughts are still considered healthy for a pregnant mother, but we know that what a mother thinks will not harm her baby.

The borning room

Settler babies were not born in hospitals. A special room, called a **borning room**, was located beside the kitchen in the family home. The heat from the kitchen stove kept the borning room cosy and warm for the mother and her child.

Bathing in wine

As soon as a baby was born, it was given a bath in wine! The early settlers believed that wine fought disease and made the baby strong. After the bath, the baby was wrapped snugly in a large flannel cloth.

How to quiet a grouchy baby

Babies who are getting new teeth are often very irritable. The early settlers had a solution for calming grouchy infants. They coated the baby's hands with molasses and gave it chicken feathers to hold. As babies tried to pull the chicken feathers off their sticky hands, they wore themselves out and fell asleep!

The naming game

Many settler children were given the names of people in the Bible. Some popular names for girls were Sarah, Mary, Ruth, and Esther. Boys were often called John, Joseph, Noah, or Daniel. Some children were named after family members or the friends of their parents. To avoid confusion, an adjective was added to the child's name. Some children had names such as "little John" or "big Anna."

Shortly after a baby was born, a **christening** *was held to name the baby and welcome him or her into the church. This baby is wearing a traditional white christening dress.*

Many settler babies slept in **bassinets.** *Sweet dreams, baby!*

27

Odds 'n' ends

Porky pollution fighters

Most animals were not allowed on public roads, but some communities made an exception for pigs. Each morning at five o'clock, pigs were let loose to eat the garbage that had gathered on the roads!

Living in the fast lane

In England, people drove on the left side of the road. The first settlers in North America also tried to drive their Conestoga wagons on the

Pigs were more than just good food for dinner. They were also early garbage-disposal units that ate litter right off the roads!

left. Unfortunately, Conestoga wagons tended to pull to the right. Wagon drivers decided that it was safer to stay on the right side of the road. That way, if something happened to the driver, the wagon would drift off the road and not hit other wagons. Today, North American drivers still drive on the right.

Leaving a nest egg

The settlers had to be very tricky with their stubborn chickens, which didn't always want to lay eggs. Children made eggs from clay and painted them with whitewash. They placed the eggs in the chicken coops and fooled the chickens into thinking it was time to start a family. The chickens then laid real eggs.

Hair receivers

The early settlers used hair for making jewelry. They also used hair as thread to embroider samplers! The hair was collected from the bristles of brushes and saved in a fancy porcelain bowl called a **hair receiver**. Hair was pushed through a hole in the bowl's lid.

Superstitious settlers

Glowing fireflies, croaking frogs, chirping crickets, and hooting owls made the night hours a spooky time for the early settlers. Many people believed in ghosts, hobgoblins, and other supernatural beings. Some people thought that white animals such as horses and sheep turned into phantoms at night. Barn owls were also believed to have supernatural powers. One of the reasons for this owl's ghostly reputation was that it was often seen in cemeteries. Its eerie screeches made settlers shiver with fright!

No, this isn't a candy dish. The settlers used fancy decorated bowls, called hair receivers, *to hold their old hair!*

The settlers believed in ghosts, goblins, and other spooky creatures. Write a story about a settler ghost who lives inside a pickle barrel at the general store!

Activities

Silhouettes

Silhouettes of family members were kept and passed down from generation to generation. A silhouette artist studied a person's profile and then cut it out of a piece of stiff black paper. The result looked like a shadow of the person's head.

You can make a silhouette of a friend or family member. Tape a piece of paper to a wall. Set up a light to shine on the paper. Have your model pose between the light and the wall so that the shadow of his or her profile is projected onto the paper. Trace the profile as your model stands very still. Carefully cut out the silhouette. Make sure you do not snip off the nose! Paste the silhouette to a sheet of different-colored paper.

Skillet-baked apples

The apple harvest was an exciting time of year for settler families. Traditions such as the apple-peeling bee were fun social events. Settlers might have enjoyed this traditional apple treat on chilly autumn evenings around the fireplace.

6 apples, cored
25 ml (5 tsp) butter
80 ml (1/2 cup) brown sugar
cinnamon to taste
100 ml (1/3 cup) water

Place cored apples in a skillet. Mix butter, sugar, and cinnamon together. Fill the apple centers with this mixture. Add water to the pan. Cover and bring to a boil. Reduce heat and simmer for half an hour until the apples are tender.

Silhouette artists were traveling artisans. They moved from village to village, creating masterpieces with their scissors and paper.

Glossary

adjective A word that describes a person, place, or thing

ale A bitter-tasting beer

artisan A craftsperson

bee A gathering in which work and fun are combined. Settlers had corn-husking bees, quilting bees, and barn-raising bees.

bran The ground inner husks of grain, sifted from flour

brooch A pin worn at the neck or shoulder for decoration

canine Describing or relating to dogs

castor oil An oil made from the seeds of a tropical plant

china Fine pottery

churn A device in which cream is beaten until butter forms

Conestoga wagon A large wagon with a covered top

dandruff Flakes of dead skin that fall from the scalp

embroider To sew decorative stitching using colored thread

fasting Not eating for a period of time

flannel A soft woolen fabric

hobgoblin An imaginary mischievous spirit

holly An evergreen shrub with prickly leaves and red berries

mustard plaster A heated mixture of mustard powder, flour, and water, which was applied to the chest to cure illnesses

nutmeg A hard fragrant tropical seed, which is ground into a powder and used as a spice

pare To peel

pestle A tool used for crushing grains

phantom A ghost

pliers A tool used for gripping or bending metal

porcelain Fine china made of white clay

Puritan A strict Christian group that originated in England. Many Puritans settled in North America.

rosemary Fragrant leaves used to add flavor to food

serenade To play music and sing to a particular person or persons

sermon A speech about religion or morals given in a church

skillet A deep, flat pan

stocks Punishment devices in which the legs were held in a wooden brace so that the criminal could not walk

supernatural Describing powers outside the forces of nature

tinker A traveling mender of pots and pans

trivet A metal stand with feet, used for supporting hot dishes over coals

values Strong beliefs about what is right and wrong

whitewash A liquid containing lime or powdered chalk

Index

Acknowledgments

Illustrations and colorizations

Barb Bedell: cover, pages 18-19 (top), 25 (bottom)
Antoinette "Cookie" DeBiasi: title page, pages 4, 6 (bottom), 13 (top), 15, 16 (top), 20, 21, 22, 23 (both), 25 (top), 26 (bottom), 29, 30
Tammy Everts: pages 7, 12, 18-19 (bottom), 26 (top), 27, 28
Karen Harrison: page 13 (bottom)
Tina Holdcroft: page 6 (top)
Rudy Irish: page 17
Debra Watton: page 11

Photographs

Jim Bryant: page 5
Marc Crabtree: page 9 (top)
Peter Crabtree: page 4
Tammy Everts: page 14
Ken Faris: page 8 (top)
Bobbie Kalman: pages 21, 29
Metropolitan Regional Conservation Authority: pages 8 (inset), 10, 20, 24 (both), 27
National Archives: page 9 (inset)

4 5 6 7 8 9 0   Printed in U.S.A.   3 2 1 0 9 8 7 6